The Insurance Handbook

A General Guide for Everyday Protection

By: Isaac Banahene Amoyaw

Table of Contents

Chapter 1

<hr>

Introduction to Insurance

What is Insurance?

Insurance is a crucial aspect of our lives that provides financial protection against unexpected events and the potential financial losses that may arise from them. Whether it's protecting your home, health, car, or business, insurance acts as a safety net, giving you peace of mind and ensuring your financial security.

At its core, insurance is a contract between an individual, known as the policyholder, and an insurance company. The policyholder pays a regular premium for coverage, usually monthly or annually. In the event of a covered loss, the insurance company agrees to compensate the policyholder for their financial losses up to the limits specified in the policy.

Various types of insurance are available, each designed to address specific needs and risks. Let's look at some common kinds of insurance:

1. Health Insurance: Provides coverage for medical expenses, including doctor visits, hospitalization, medications, and preventive care. It helps individuals manage the rising healthcare costs and ensures access to quality medical services.

2. Homeowners Insurance: Protects your home and personal belongings against damage or loss caused by fire, theft, vandalism, or natural disasters. It also provides liability coverage in case someone is injured on your property.

3. Auto Insurance: This covers damages to your vehicle and any liability arising from accidents. It is a legal requirement in most places and helps protect you financially from the high costs of repairs, medical bills, and legal expenses.

4. Life Insurance: Provides financial support to your loved ones during your death. It can help cover funeral expenses, pay off

outstanding debts, and provide income replacement for your family.

5. Business Insurance: Protects businesses from financial losses due to property damage, liability claims, or interruptions in operations. It can include coverage for property, general liability, professional liability, and more.

Understanding the basics of insurance is essential for everyone. It helps individuals and businesses make informed decisions about the types and amounts of coverage they need. By transferring risk to an insurance company, you can protect yourself and your assets from unforeseen circumstances that may otherwise have a significant financial impact.

Remember, insurance is not just an expense but an investment in your financial security and peace of mind. By choosing the right coverage and understanding the terms and conditions of your policy, you can ensure that you are adequately protected in times of need.

History of Insurance

Insurance has become integral to our lives today, providing us with protection and peace of mind in uncertain times. However, the concept of insurance has a long and fascinating history that dates back centuries. Understanding the roots and evolution of insurance can provide us with a deeper appreciation for the industry that safeguards our belongings, health, and financial stability.

The origins of insurance can be traced back to ancient civilizations, such as the Babylonians and Chinese. Merchants and traders formed mutual agreements in these early societies to protect their goods during long and dangerous journeys. This practice laid the foundation for what we now know as marine insurance.

The concept of insurance gained further traction during the Middle Ages when guilds and fraternities emerged. These organizations provided financial support to members who faced unexpected events like fire, theft, or illness. The idea of pooling resources to mitigate individual risks became increasingly popular.

The modern insurance industry as we know it today began to take shape in the 17th century. 1666, the Great Fire of London led to significant property damage and financial losses. This catastrophic event prompted the establishment of the first fire insurance company, which protected against fire-related risks.

Insurance continued to evolve during the 18th and 19th centuries, with the emergence of various types of coverage. Life insurance, initially seen as a form of investment, gained prominence as a means to provide for families in the event of a breadwinner's untimely death. Other forms of insurance, such as property and casualty, also became more prevalent during this time.

In the 20th century, we witnessed significant advancements in the insurance industry. Introducing automobile insurance helped address the risks associated with the increasing number of cars on the road. Additionally, the advent of technology and global trade gave rise to specialized forms of insurance, including cyber insurance and international shipping coverage.

Today, insurance plays a crucial role in our daily lives, protecting a wide range of risks. Whether it is safeguarding our homes, businesses, health, or vehicles, insurance offers a safety net for individuals and society. The industry continues to adapt and innovate, embracing new technologies and expanding its offerings to meet the ever-changing needs of individuals and businesses.

Understanding insurance history allows us to appreciate the immense progress made over the centuries. It reminds us of the importance of insurance in mitigating risks and promoting stability in an unpredictable world. As we navigate the complexities of modern life, insurance remains a vital tool for everyday protection.

Importance of Insurance in Everyday Life

Insurance provides peace of mind and financial security in an uncertain world. Whether it's protecting your health, home, car, or loved ones, insurance is an essential tool that safeguards you from unexpected events and helps you bounce back when the unexpected strikes. This subchapter explores the importance of insurance in our everyday lives and highlights the key reasons why insurance is crucial for individuals across all walks of life.

One of the primary reasons insurances is essential is its ability to protect our most valuable assets. For instance, homeowners' insurance shields us from the financial burden of property damage caused by natural disasters, accidents, or theft. Similarly, auto insurance ensures that we are covered in case of accidents, providing financial support to repair or replace our vehicles. These unforeseen events could cause severe financial strain without insurance, potentially leading to bankruptcy or significant debt.

Additionally, insurance plays a crucial role in safeguarding our health and well-being. Health insurance allows individuals to access quality medical care without worrying about excessive costs. It covers hospitalisation expenses, routine check-ups, medications, and specialized treatments. By having health insurance, individuals can focus on their recovery and well-being rather than the financial burden of medical bills.

Another aspect of insurance that shouldn't be overlooked is the protection it offers to our loved ones. Life insurance ensures that your family is financially secure during your untimely demise. It provides a safety net to cover funeral expenses, outstanding debts, and loss of income, allowing your family to maintain their standard of living during a difficult time.

Moreover, insurance promotes a sense of responsibility and risk management. With insurance, individuals are encouraged to take precautions and implement safety measures to prevent accidents and mitigate risks. Insurance providers often offer resources and guidance on minimising hazards, creating a safer and more secure environment for everyone involved.

In conclusion, insurance is an indispensable part of our everyday lives. Its importance cannot be underestimated as it protects our assets, provides financial security during times of crisis, and ensures the well-being of our loved ones. By understanding the various types of insurance available and obtaining appropriate coverage, individuals can proactively safeguard themselves from potential risks and enjoy the peace of mind that comes with knowing they are protected.

Chapter 2

Understanding Insurance Policies

Types of Insurance Policies

Insurance is a vital component of our lives, providing financial protection against unexpected events and minimizing the potential risks we face. However, navigating the insurance world can be overwhelming with the vast array of insurance policies available. This subchapter will explore various insurance policies to address specific needs and risks.

1. Health Insurance: This policy covers medical expenses and provides financial support for hospitalization, doctor visits, prescription medications, and surgical procedures. Health insurance offers peace of mind, ensuring access to quality healthcare without exorbitant expenses.

2. Auto Insurance: Mandatory in most countries, auto insurance protects against

financial loss due to accidents, theft, or damage to your vehicle. It offers liability coverage, medical payments, and personal injury protection, safeguarding you against potential lawsuits and providing coverage for repairs or vehicle replacement.

3. Homeowners Insurance: This policy protects your home against damage caused by natural disasters, fire, theft, or vandalism. It also covers personal belongings and liability coverage if someone gets injured on your property. Homeowners insurance is essential for safeguarding your most significant investment.

4. Life Insurance: Life insurance ensures financial security for your loved ones during your death. It provides a lump sum payment to beneficiaries, helping cover funeral expenses, outstanding debts, and ongoing living expenses. It can be term life insurance, which provides coverage for a specific term, or permanent life insurance, which covers your entire life.

5. Disability Insurance: This policy replaces income if you cannot work due to a disability or illness. It ensures you can maintain your

lifestyle and meet financial obligations during challenging times.

6.   Travel Insurance: Travel insurance protects against unforeseen travel events, including trip cancellation, medical emergencies, lost luggage, or delays. It offers peace of mind, so you can enjoy your trips without worrying about unexpected expenses.

These are just a few examples of the many insurance policies available to mitigate risks and protect your financial well-being. It is essential to assess your needs and consult with insurance professionals to determine the policies best fit your circumstances. Remember, insurance is an investment in your future, offering the security and peace of mind you and your loved ones deserve.

Life Insurance

Life insurance is a crucial aspect of financial planning that provides protection and peace of mind to individuals and their loved ones. This subchapter will delve into the ins and outs of life insurance, explaining its importance, types, and benefits.

Life insurance is a contract between an individual and an insurance company, where the company promises to pay the beneficiaries a designated sum of money, known as the death benefit, upon the insured's death. This financial protection ensures that loved ones are cared for in the event of the policyholder's untimely demise.

Several life insurance policies are available, catering to different needs and circumstances. Term life insurance is the most basic and affordable option, providing coverage for a specified term, usually 10, 20, or 30 years. On the other hand, whole life insurance offers lifelong coverage and accumulates cash value over time. Different variations include universal and variable life insurance, which offers flexibility and investment options.

The benefits of having life insurance are manifold. Firstly, it provides a safety net for dependents, ensuring they are financially secure even after the policyholder's passing. The death benefit can cover funeral expenses, outstanding debts, mortgage payments, and other financial obligations. Additionally, life insurance can be an inheritance for loved ones, providing them with a financial legacy.

Another advantage of life insurance is its tax benefits. In most cases, the death benefit is tax-free, meaning beneficiaries receive the total amount without tax liabilities. Furthermore, some life insurance policies offer cash value growth, allowing policyholders to access funds during their lifetime for emergencies, education expenses, or retirement planning.

When considering life insurance, it's essential to assess your needs and budget carefully. Age, health, income, and financial goals should be considered. It is recommended to consult with a licensed insurance agent or financial advisor who can provide personalized guidance and help you choose the most suitable policy.

In conclusion, life insurance is vital in safeguarding your loved one's financial future. By choosing the right type and amount of coverage, you can have peace of mind knowing that your family will be protected in your absence. So, don't delay securing your loved ones' future – explore the world of life insurance and make an informed decision today.

Health Insurance

Health insurance is crucial to safeguarding individuals' and families' well-being and financial stability. This subchapter will explore the various aspects of health insurance, its importance, and how it functions today.

Health insurance is a type of insurance coverage that pays for medical and surgical expenses incurred by the insured. It provides financial protection against high healthcare costs, including doctor visits, hospital stays, prescription medications, and other medical services. By obtaining health insurance, individuals can access quality healthcare without worrying about the financial burden it may impose.

One of the fundamental components of health insurance is the premium, which is the amount paid by the insured regularly to maintain coverage. The premium is determined based on age, health status, location, and the level of coverage desired. It is essential for individuals to carefully review and compare different health insurance plans to find one that suits their specific needs and budget.

Health insurance plans typically come in two main categories: private and government-sponsored health insurance. Private health insurance can be obtained through employers, professional associations, or purchased individually. Government-sponsored health insurance programs, such as Medicare and Medicaid, are designed to cover specific populations, including the elderly, low-income individuals, and disabled individuals.

Understanding health insurance terms and concepts is crucial for making informed decisions. Key terms to be familiar with include deductibles, co-payments, and co-insurance. Deductibles are the amount individuals must pay out of pocket before the insurance coverage kicks in. Co-payments refer to the fixed amount individuals must pay for each visit or service, while co-insurance is the percentage individuals are responsible for paying after meeting the deductible.

It is important to note that health insurance plans often have limitations and exclusions. These include pre-existing conditions, certain treatments or medications, and specific healthcare providers. It is essential to thoroughly review the policy documentation to understand what is covered and what is not entirely.

In conclusion, health insurance is a vital component of everyday protection. It provides individuals and families with financial security and access to quality healthcare. By understanding the various aspects of health insurance and carefully selecting the right plan, individuals can ensure their well-being and peace of mind in medical need.

Property Insurance

Introduction:

Property insurance is a crucial aspect of everyday protection, providing individuals and businesses with coverage against potential losses or damages to their properties. Whether you own a home, a commercial building, or other valuable assets, having the right property insurance policy can provide you with peace of mind and financial security. This subchapter aims to provide a general guide to property insurance, explaining its importance, types of coverage, and factors to consider when selecting a policy.

Understanding Property Insurance:

Property insurance protects your investments by covering the costs of repairing or replacing damaged or destroyed properties. This insurance coverage typically includes protection against risks such as fire, theft, natural disasters, and vandalism. By paying regular premiums, policyholders can transfer the financial burden of potential losses to the insurance company.

Types of Property Insurance Coverage:

Property insurance policies come in various forms, offering coverage for multiple assets. The most common types of property insurance include homeowners' insurance, renters insurance, and commercial property insurance. Homeowners insurance protects homeowners against property damage and liability, while renters' insurance covers tenants' personal belongings. On the other hand, commercial property insurance protects businesses and organizations against property damage, business interruption, and liability claims.

Factors to Consider when Selecting a Policy:

When choosing a property insurance policy, it is essential to consider several factors. These include the value of your property, the location, the risks associated with the area, and the coverage limits and deductibles offered by the policy. Additionally, it is crucial to review the terms and conditions, exclusions, and any additional coverage options available. Comparing quotes from different insurance providers and seeking professional advice can help you make an informed decision.

Conclusion:

Property insurance is essential to everyday protection, providing individuals and businesses with financial security against potential property losses. Understanding the various types of coverage available and considering key factors when selecting a policy can ensure you have the right level of protection for your valuable assets. Investing in property insurance can mitigate the financial risks associated with property damage or loss, allowing you to focus on other aspects of your life or business with peace of mind. Remember, it is always advisable to consult with an insurance professional to assess your needs and find the most suitable property insurance policy.

Auto Insurance

Auto insurance is a crucial aspect of everyday protection for individuals who own and operate vehicles. Whether you drive a car, truck, motorcycle, or any other type of motor vehicle, having adequate auto insurance coverage is a legal requirement in most jurisdictions and a wise financial decision.

Auto insurance provides financial protection against damages or losses resulting from accidents, theft, vandalism, or other unfortunate events involving your vehicle. It helps cover the costs of repairs, medical expenses, legal fees, and even vehicle replacement, depending on the coverage you choose.

Several types of auto insurance coverage are available, including liability coverage, collision coverage, comprehensive coverage, uninsured/underinsured motorist coverage, and personal injury protection (PIP). Understanding each type of coverage and selecting the appropriate combination can ensure you have the right level of protection tailored to your needs.

Liability coverage is typically the minimum requirement in most jurisdictions. It covers damages and injuries you cause to others in an accident. Collision coverage, on the other hand, pays for damages to your vehicle in case of a collision, regardless of fault. Comprehensive coverage protects against non-collision incidents like theft, vandalism, or natural disasters.

Uninsured/underinsured motorist coverage is designed to protect you if you are involved in an accident with a driver who does not have insurance or does not have enough coverage to pay for your damages. Personal injury protection (PIP) covers medical expenses and lost wages for you and your passengers, regardless of who is at fault.

When purchasing auto insurance, it is essential to consider factors such as the value of your vehicle, your driving record, your location, and any additional coverage you may need. Comparing quotes from multiple insurers can help you find the best coverage at the most affordable price.

Remember, auto insurance protects your financial well-being and provides peace of mind while on the road. It ensures you are prepared for unexpected events and can recover from potential losses without a significant financial burden.

In conclusion, auto insurance is a vital component of everyday protection for vehicle owners. By understanding the different types of coverage available and selecting the right combination for your needs, you can drive confidently, knowing you are financially protected against potential risks and losses.

Liability Insurance

Liability insurance is crucial to protecting yourself and your assets in today's litigious society. Whether you are a business owner, homeowner, or a responsible individual, understanding liability insurance basics is essential for your financial security and peace of mind.

Liability insurance covers any legal obligations or financial responsibilities you may incur if you are found legally liable for causing injury or property damage to another person. This type of insurance protects you from the potentially devastating financial consequences of a lawsuit or legal claim.

Liability insurance is critical for businesses as it can safeguard against claims arising from accidents, negligence, or other unforeseen circumstances. General liability insurance, for example, provides coverage for bodily injury, property damage, and personal injury claims that may occur on your business premises or because of your business operations. This coverage can also extend to product liability claims, ensuring that you are protected if someone is injured or suffers damages due to a faulty product you manufacture or sell.

Homeowners also benefit from liability insurance, as it shields them from costly legal expenses and damages resulting from accidents on their property. Suppose someone slips and falls in your driveway or a tree from your yard falls and damages a neighbour's property. In that case, liability insurance can help cover the costs of medical bills, legal fees, and property repairs.

Even individuals without a business or homeownership can benefit from liability insurance. Personal liability insurance protects in situations where you may be held responsible for causing harm to another person or their property. This can include incidents like a car accident, where you may be liable for the injuries or damages incurred by others involved in the accident.

Understanding liability insurance and its importance is essential for anyone concerned about protecting their financial well-being. With the right liability insurance coverage, you can rest easy knowing that you are shielded from the potentially devastating economic consequences of a lawsuit or legal claim.

In conclusion, liability insurance is a crucial component of everyday protection. Whether you are a business owner, homeowner, or an individual, having liability insurance ensures that you are financially secure in case of a lawsuit or legal claim. By understanding liability insurance basics, you can make informed decisions when selecting the appropriate coverage to suit your needs. Accidents happen, and being adequately insured can offer you the peace of mind you deserve in today's litigious world.

Key Terms and Definitions in Insurance Policies

Understanding insurance policies and their terminology is crucial for anyone seeking protection in their everyday lives. Insurance policies provide financial security and peace of mind, Whether for your home, car, health, or any other aspect of your life. This subchapter will explore critical terms and definitions commonly found in insurance policies, ensuring you have a solid foundation for making informed decisions regarding your insurance needs.

1. Premium: The amount you pay the insurance company for coverage. Premiums can be paid annually, semi-annually, quarterly, or monthly, depending on the policy and the insurer's terms.

2. Deductible: The portion of a claim you must pay out of pocket before your insurance coverage kicks in. Higher deductibles usually result in lower premiums, while lower deductibles mean higher premiums.

3. Coverage limit: The maximum amount an insurance company will pay for a covered claim. It is essential to understand the

coverage limits of your policy to ensure adequate protection.

4. Policyholder: The person who owns the insurance policy and is entitled to the benefits and coverage outlined in the policy.

5. Insured: The person or property covered by the insurance policy. This can include yourself, your family members, or any other individuals or assets specified in the policy.

6. Claim: A request made by the policyholder to the insurance company for financial compensation due to a loss or damage covered by the policy. Claims are typically subject to investigation and approval by the insurance company.

7. Exclusion: Specific situations or events not covered by the insurance policy. You are reviewing the exclusions to fully understand what is included and excluded from your coverage, which is crucial.

8. Rider: Also known as an endorsement, a rider is an additional provision or coverage added to the primary insurance policy to tailor it to your needs. This can include coverage for high-value items, additional

liability protection, or coverage for specific events.

9. Policy term: The period during which the insurance policy is in effect. It is essential to review the policy term to ensure continuous coverage and to avoid any gaps in protection.

10. Insurer: The insurance company that provides coverage and assumes the financial risk in the event of a claim.

By familiarizing yourself with these key terms and definitions, you will be better equipped to understand the language used in insurance policies. This knowledge will empower you to make informed decisions about your insurance coverage, ensuring you have the proper protection for your needs. Review your policy thoroughly and consult a licensed insurance professional for clarification or questions.

Choosing the Right Insurance Policy for Your Needs

Having the right insurance policy is crucial when protecting yourself and your assets. With the wide range of insurance options available today, determining which policy best suits your needs can be overwhelming.

This subchapter aims to guide you through choosing the right insurance policy, ensuring you make an informed decision providing adequate coverage.

Before diving into the various insurance policies available, it is essential to assess your specific needs. Consider the risks you face, the assets you want to protect, and any potential liabilities you may have. For instance, if you own a home, homeowner's insurance will be a priority, while auto insurance is necessary for vehicle owners. By identifying these needs, you can narrow down the types of insurance policies to focus on.

Once you have identified your needs, it's time to familiarize yourself with the different insurance policies available. Some common types include life insurance, health insurance, homeowner's or renter's insurance, auto insurance, and business insurance. Each policy serves a specific purpose and offers coverage in different areas. Understanding the coverage and limitations of each policy will help you make an informed decision regarding your insurance needs.

Comparing different insurance providers is essential to ensure you choose the right policy. Look for reputable insurers with a solid financial standing and a track record of excellent customer service. Request quotes from multiple insurers and carefully review the coverage details, deductibles, and premiums. Don't hesitate to ask questions and seek clarification on any areas that may be unclear to you.

Additionally, consider seeking advice from insurance brokers or agents who specialize in the specific type of insurance you require. They can provide valuable insights and help you navigate the complex world of insurance policies. Remember, the goal is to find a policy that offers comprehensive coverage at a reasonable price.

Lastly, regularly review and reassess your insurance needs. As your circumstances change, so too will your insurance requirements. Whether you experience significant life events, such as getting married, having children, starting a business, or want to ensure adequate coverage periodically, evaluating and updating your insurance policies is essential.

Choosing the right insurance policy for your needs may seem daunting, but with careful consideration and research, you can make an informed decision. By understanding your specific requirements, comparing policies, and seeking professional advice, when necessary, you can ensure that you have the right insurance coverage to protect yourself, your loved ones, and your assets.

Chapter 3

Insurance Coverage and Claims

Coverage Limits and Deductibles

Understanding the terms and conditions of your insurance policy is crucial to ensure you have adequate protection for your valuable assets and personal well-being. Coverage limits and deductibles are critical when choosing an insurance policy. Let's delve into these concepts to help you make informed decisions regarding your insurance needs.

Coverage limits refer to the maximum amount an insurance company will pay for a covered loss or claim. These limits vary depending on your insurance type, such as auto, home, or health insurance. It is essential to carefully review your policy to understand the specific coverage limits for each category.

When determining the appropriate coverage limits for your insurance policy, you must evaluate your circumstances and the potential risks you face. Consider factors such as the value of your assets, your income, and any potential liability you may have. It is generally advisable to select coverage limits that adequately protect your investments and potential future earnings.

Additionally, insurance policies often include deductibles. A deductible is the amount you must pay out of pocket before your insurance coverage kicks in. For example, if you have a $500 deductible on your auto insurance policy and are involved in an accident resulting in $2, 000 in damages, you would be responsible for paying the first $500, and the insurance company would cover the remaining $1, 500.

Deductibles serve two primary purposes. First, they help to reduce the number of small claims that insurance companies must process, allowing them to focus on more significant losses. Second, they encourage policyholders to exercise caution and minimize risks, as they bear a portion of the financial burden.

When selecting a deductible, balancing affordability and financial protection is essential. Higher deductibles typically result in lower premiums, but they also require you to pay more out of pocket in the event of a claim. Conversely, lower deductibles offer more immediate financial relief but may increase premiums.

Understanding coverage limits and deductibles is vital to ensure you have the proper insurance protection that fits your needs and budget. Take the time to review your policy, consult with insurance professionals, and assess your circumstances. By doing so, you can make informed decisions and secure the peace of mind that comes with having the appropriate insurance coverage.

How Insurance Claims Work

Understanding the process of insurance claims is essential for anyone seeking to protect their assets and investments. This subchapter will delve into how insurance claims work, providing a general guide for individuals seeking everyday protection through insurance.

When an unforeseen event results in damage or loss to your insured property, the first step is to notify your insurance company about the incident. This can typically be done through a phone call or an online portal. Reporting the claim as soon as possible ensures a smooth and efficient process.

After reporting the claim, an insurance adjuster will be assigned to your case. The adjuster's role is to investigate the claim, assess the damage, and determine the coverage available under your insurance policy. They may also ask for supporting documentation such as photographs, police reports, or medical records, depending on the nature of the claim.

Once the investigation is complete, the insurance company will evaluate the claim and decide whether to approve or deny it. The insurer will provide compensation based on the policy terms and conditions if approved. The payment amount will depend on factors such as the extent of damage, the deductible, and any applicable limits or exclusions mentioned in the policy.

It is worth noting that insurance claims are subject to deductibles, which are predetermined amounts that policyholders are responsible for paying before the insurance coverage kicks in. The deductible can vary depending on the type of insurance and the specific policy details.

The insurance company may sometimes require the policyholder to obtain repair estimates or seek medical evaluations from approved professionals. This ensures that the claim is handled accurately, and that the insurer is not overpaying for the damages.

If a claim is denied, policyholders can appeal the decision or seek legal advice to explore their rights and options. Understanding the terms and conditions of your insurance policy beforehand can help prevent claim denials and ensure that you have adequate coverage for potential losses.

In summary, navigating the world of insurance claims requires a proactive approach and understanding of how the process works. Policyholders can increase their chances of a successful resolution by promptly reporting a claim, providing necessary documentation, and cooperating with the insurance adjuster. Remember, insurance protects you from unexpected events, and a thorough understanding of the claims process is crucial for obtaining the necessary coverage.

Tips for Filing an Insurance Claim

Filing an insurance claim can be daunting, especially if you have never done it before. However, the process can be much smoother and less stressful with the proper knowledge and preparation. This subchapter will provide valuable tips on filing an insurance claim effectively and efficiently.

1. Understand your policy: Reviewing your insurance policy thoroughly is crucial before filing a claim. Familiarize yourself with the coverage limits, deductibles, and exclusions. This will help you clearly understand what is covered and what is not, preventing any surprises during the claims process.

2. Document everything: When filing a claim, documentation is critical. Take pictures or videos of the damage or loss, write detailed descriptions, and gather supporting evidence, such as receipts or invoices. This evidence will strengthen your claim and make it easier for the insurance company to assess the situation accurately.

3. Notify your insurance company promptly: Informing them about the incident as soon as possible is essential. Most insurance policies have a specific time frame within which you must report a claim. Failure to do so may result in a denial of your claim.

4. Be honest and accurate: Always be truthful and precise when providing information to your insurance company. Any misrepresentation or false information can lead to severe consequences, including claim denial or even policy cancellation. Stick to the facts and provide any necessary documentation to support your claim.

5. Keep records of communication: Throughout the claims process, maintain a record of all communications with your insurance company. This includes emails, phone calls, and any other correspondence. Keeping a record will help you stay organized and provide evidence of any agreements or promises made during the process.

6. Follow up regularly: Insurance claims can sometimes take time to process. Regularly following up with your insurance company ensures your claim is moving forward. Be

polite but persistent in your communication to stay informed about the progress of your claim.

7. Seek professional help if needed: If you struggle with the claims process or face difficulties, consider seeking professional help. Insurance brokers or public adjusters can provide valuable expertise and guidance to ensure you receive fair compensation.

Remember, filing an insurance claim is your right as a policyholder, and you deserve to be treated fairly. By following these tips and staying organized throughout the process, you can navigate the claims process more effectively and increase your chances of a successful outcome.

Common Mistakes to Avoid in Insurance Claims

When filing insurance claims, individuals often make several common mistakes. These mistakes can result in delays, denials, or reduced payouts, leaving policyholders frustrated and financially burdened. In this subchapter, we will highlight some of the most common mistakes to avoid when filing insurance claims, ensuring that you have a smooth and successful claims process.

One of the most significant mistakes people make is understanding their insurance policy. Reading and comprehending your policy's terms, conditions, and coverage limits is crucial. Without a clear understanding of what is covered and what is not, you may inadvertently file a claim for something excluded, resulting in its rejection.

Another mistake to avoid is delaying reporting an incident to your insurance provider. Notifying your insurer immediately after an accident, damage, or loss has occurred is essential. Waiting too long may give the impression that the incident was insignificant or could even be interpreted as fraud, leading to complications and potential denial of your claim.

Underestimating the value of your belongings is another common mistake. Many policyholders fail to accurately assess the worth of their possessions, resulting in insufficient coverage. Take the time to document your assets and their estimated value regularly. This will ensure adequate coverage in case of loss or damage.

Filing incomplete or inaccurate claim forms is yet another mistake to avoid. When filling out claim forms, accurately provide all requested information. Missing or incorrect data can delay the processing of your claim or even its denial.

Lastly, avoiding settling for less than what you deserve is essential. Insurance companies may try to minimize payouts, mainly if you are unaware of your rights or the full extent of your coverage. Seek professional advice and negotiate with your insurer to ensure you receive a fair and just settlement.

Awareness of these common mistakes and taking proactive steps to avoid them can significantly enhance your chances of a successful insurance claim. Remember to understand your policy thoroughly, report incidents promptly, accurately assess the value of your belongings, fill out claim forms meticulously, and advocate for fair compensation. By doing so, you will be well-equipped to navigate the claims process and protect your financial well-being.

Chapter 4

Assessing Insurance Risks

Identifying Potential Risks in Life

Life is full of uncertainties, and no one is immune to unexpected events that can turn our lives upside down. Whether it's a sudden illness, a natural disaster, or an unfortunate accident, the possibility of facing unforeseen challenges is always present. That's why it is crucial to identify potential risks and take proactive measures to protect ourselves and our loved ones. This subchapter will explore the importance of identifying potential threats in life and how insurance can play a vital role in providing everyday protection.

The first step in managing risks is understanding the various areas where we might be vulnerable. This includes our health, property, income, and lives. By analysing potential dangers in these areas, we can make informed decisions about what kind of insurance coverage we need. For example, if you are the primary breadwinner in your family, life insurance can provide financial security to your dependents in the event of your untimely demise. Similarly, health insurance can safeguard against exorbitant medical treatments and hospitalization costs.

Another crucial aspect to consider is property insurance. Your home, car, and other valuable assets are susceptible to damage or loss due to fire, accidents, theft, or natural disasters. Having the right property insurance coverage can mitigate the financial burden of such incidents and ensure you can rebuild your life without undue stress.

Furthermore, evaluating potential risks specific to your occupation or business is essential. Are you adequately insured against potential liabilities? As a business owner, do you have coverage for potential legal claims, employee injury, or property damage? Understanding the potential risks in your professional life and securing the appropriate insurance policies can safeguard your business and personal assets.

In conclusion, identifying potential risks in life is the first step towards protecting ourselves from unforeseen circumstances. By understanding the hazards associated with our health, property, income, and occupation, we can make informed decisions about the required insurance coverage. Insurance is a safety net providing financial protection and peace of mind. Whether you are a general audience or have specific insurance needs, being aware of potential risks and having the appropriate insurance coverage is essential for everyday protection.

Evaluating Risks in Health and Wellness

In today's fast-paced world, maintaining good health and wellness is of paramount importance. However, unforeseen events can sometimes disrupt our well-being, making it essential to have a comprehensive insurance plan in place. This subchapter, "Evaluating Risks in Health and Wellness, " aims to provide a general understanding of assessing potential risks and making informed decisions regarding insurance coverage.

When evaluating risks in health and wellness, it is crucial to consider various factors.

Firstly, assess your individual health needs and lifestyle choices. Consider your age, pre-existing medical conditions, and any potential health risks associated with your occupation or hobbies. Understanding your unique circumstances allows you to identify the specific coverage options that best suit your situation.

Next, it is essential to evaluate your financial capabilities. Consider your budget and determine what you can afford in premiums and out-of-pocket expenses. Balancing cost versus coverage is a critical aspect of assessing risks in health and wellness. Remember that insurance is an investment in your future well-being, so finding the right balance is vital.

Furthermore, consider the potential risks associated with your geographic location. Certain areas may be prone to specific health issues or natural disasters, impacting your insurance needs. For example, individuals living in flood-prone regions may require additional coverage to protect against property damage and potential health risks associated with flooding.

When evaluating insurance options, thoroughly research different policies and their coverage details. Consider the extent of coverage for routine check-ups, preventive care, hospitalizations, and specialized treatments. Understanding each policy's limitations, exclusions, and waiting periods is crucial. This level of understanding will enable you to make an informed decision and ensure that you are adequately covered for potential risks.

Lastly, seek professional advice. Insurance agents and brokers specialize in providing guidance and support in navigating the complex landscape of health and wellness insurance. Their expertise can help you evaluate risks, understand policy terms, and find the most suitable coverage for your unique circumstances.

In conclusion, evaluating risks in health and wellness is a crucial step in securing optimal insurance coverage. By considering individual health needs, financial capabilities, and geographical factors and thoroughly researching options, individuals can make informed decisions to protect their well-being. Remember, insurance is an investment in your future, providing peace of mind and financial security during unexpected health challenges.

Assessing Property and Home Risks

When protecting your property and home, it is crucial to understand the various risks that can potentially cause damage or loss. Assessing these risks is essential in obtaining the right insurance coverage to safeguard your valuable assets. This subchapter will provide you with insights on how to determine property and home risks effectively.

One of the first aspects to consider when assessing property risks is the location. Different regions are prone to specific hazards, such as hurricanes, earthquakes, floods, or wildfires. Understanding the likelihood of these events occurring in your area will help you determine the appropriate coverage to protect your property against them.

Next, evaluating your home's construction and structural elements is essential. Older houses may have outdated electrical systems or plumbing, increasing the risk of fire or water damage. Furthermore, the construction materials can affect a property's vulnerability to specific perils. Assessing these factors will enable you to identify potential risks and take appropriate measures to reduce them.

Additionally, it is crucial to evaluate the security measures in place. Installing security systems, fire alarms, and surveillance cameras can significantly reduce the risk of theft or property damage. Insurance companies often offer discounts for such security enhancements, so these investments are worth considering.

Regular maintenance is another critical aspect of risk assessment. Inspecting your property regularly allows you to identify and address potential issues before they become significant problems. For instance, checking the roof for leaks or inspecting the foundation for cracks can prevent water damage or structural issues.

Understanding the value of your property and its contents is essential for accurate insurance coverage. Conducting a comprehensive inventory of your belongings will help you determine the appropriate coverage limits. Remember to update this inventory regularly as you acquire new items or make significant changes to your property.

Lastly, don't forget to assess your personal liability risks. Homeowners' insurance typically includes liability coverage, protecting you against lawsuits resulting from accidents or injuries on your property. Evaluating potential hazards and taking preventive measures is crucial to mitigate liability risks effectively.

Assessing property and home risks is an ongoing process. As circumstances change, so do the risks associated with your property. Regularly reviewing your insurance coverage and reassessing the potential hazards will ensure you stay adequately protected. Remember, insurance is a vital tool for safeguarding your property and providing you with peace of mind.

Analysing Auto and Transportation Risks

Introduction:

This subchapter will delve into the intricacies of analysing auto and transportation risks. Understanding these risks is crucial for both insurance professionals and the public. Whether you are a car owner, a driver, or someone interested in insurance, this section will provide valuable insights into auto and transportation risks.

Auto Risks:

Automobiles are an integral part of our lives but also have inherent risks. Accidents, thefts, and damages are common dangers of owning and operating a vehicle. Insurance professionals carefully analyses these risks to determine appropriate coverage and premiums. They assess the driver's age and experience, the car's make and model, location, and even their driving history. By analysing these risks, insurers can calculate the likelihood of accidents or other incidents and offer suitable insurance policies.

Transportation Risks:

While automobiles are a significant part of transportation risks, broader considerations exist to explore. Transportation risks extend beyond individual cars to encompass various modes of transportation, such as trucks, motorcycles, trains, ships, and aeroplanes. Insurance professionals' analyses transportation risks on a larger scale, considering factors like cargo, passengers, routes, and environmental conditions. For example, when ensuring a shipping company, insurers will evaluate the potential risks associated with transporting goods over long distances, including the likelihood of damage, theft, or natural disasters.

Risk Prevention and Mitigation:

Analysing auto and transportation risks is not limited to insurance professionals. As a car owner or driver, understanding these risks can help you take necessary precautions to prevent accidents and minimize potential damages. Individuals can mitigate auto risks through regular vehicle maintenance, defensive driving techniques, and adherence to traffic laws. Additionally, transportation companies can implement safety protocols, conduct regular inspections, and provide training to their employees to reduce transportation risks.

Conclusion:

Analysing auto and transportation risks is an essential part of the insurance industry and an invaluable tool for individuals seeking appropriate coverage. By understanding the risks associated with automobiles and different modes of transportation, insurance professionals and the public can make informed decisions to protect themselves and their assets. Whether you are an insurance enthusiast or a concerned car owner, this subchapter provides a comprehensive overview of the crucial aspects to consider when analysing auto and transportation risks.

Understanding Liability Risks

Liability risks are an essential aspect of insurance coverage that everyone should be familiar with. This subchapter will delve into the various parts of liability risks and how they can impact our everyday lives. Understanding liability risks is crucial whether you are a homeowner, a business owner, or want to protect yourself from potential lawsuits.

Liability risks refer to the potential legal obligations that individuals, businesses, or organizations may face if their actions or negligence cause harm to others. These risks can arise in various situations, such as accidents, property damage, personal injuries, or defamation. Without adequate insurance coverage, individuals and businesses could face significant financial burdens or even bankruptcy due to liability claims.

For homeowners, liability risks can arise from incidents on their property, such as slip and fall accidents or dog bites. Understanding how to mitigate these risks by maintaining a safe environment and obtaining appropriate insurance coverage is vital to protect the homeowner and visitors.

On the other hand, business owners face a wide range of liability risks. These include product liability if a faulty product causes harm, professional liability for errors or omissions in services provided, or general liability for accidents on their premises. Business owners must assess risks and obtain comprehensive insurance coverage tailored to their industry and operations.

Understanding liability risks also extends to individuals and their everyday activities. For instance, you may be liable for damages if you accidentally cause a car accident or injure someone while participating in recreational activities. Personal liability insurance can cover such incidents and protect your financial well-being.

Furthermore, this subchapter will explore the importance of umbrella insurance policies. These policies offer an additional layer of liability coverage beyond the limits of your primary insurance policies. They can be particularly beneficial for individuals with substantial assets or businesses with higher exposure to liability risks.

In today's litigious society, understanding liability risks and having appropriate insurance coverage is more critical than ever. By being aware of the potential risks and taking proactive steps to mitigate them, individuals and businesses can protect themselves financially and ensure peace of mind. This subchapter will provide valuable insights and practical tips to help you navigate the complex world of liability risks and insurance coverage.

Chapter 5

Insurance Providers and Regulations

Types of Insurance Providers

Insurance is a crucial aspect of everyday life when protecting oneself and one's belongings. There are various types of insurance providers in the market today, each offering different policies and coverage options tailored to meet the diverse needs of individuals and businesses. Understanding the different types of insurance providers can help you make informed decisions when choosing the right insurance coverage for your specific requirements.

1. Insurance Companies: These are the most common insurance providers. They are private companies that offer a wide range of insurance policies such as auto, home, health, life, and business insurance. Insurance companies assess risks and determine premiums based on age, location,

and past claims history. They typically have a network of agents who help individuals and businesses select the appropriate policies and provide customer service.

2. Government Insurance Providers: Some insurance options are provided by government entities. For example, the Federal Housing Administration (FHA) offers mortgage insurance in the United States, while the National Flood Insurance Program (NFIP) provides flood insurance. These government agencies aim to provide affordable coverage and protect individuals and communities from specific risks.

3. Mutual Insurance Companies: These are owned by policyholders, not shareholders. Mutual insurance companies operate cooperatively, with policyholders sharing the risks and rewards. They often offer lower premiums and better customer service because they focus on policyholder satisfaction rather than maximizing profits.

4. Captive Insurance Companies: These insurance providers are owned and operated by businesses to provide coverage exclusively to their companies. Captive insurance companies give corporations more

control over their insurance policies and costs, allowing them to tailor coverage to their unique risks and potentially reduce premiums.

5. Reinsurance Companies: Reinsurers provide insurance to insurance companies. They help spread the risk of significant losses across multiple insurers, ensuring that no single company is overwhelmed by a catastrophic event or excessive claims. Reinsurance companies are critical in stabilizing the insurance industry and enabling insurers to offer higher coverage limits.

6. Online Insurance Providers: With the advancement of technology, many insurance providers now offer their services online. These digital insurance companies allow individuals to compare policies, obtain quotes, and purchase coverage entirely online. This convenient option is trendy among tech-savvy individuals who prefer a streamlined, self-directed insurance experience.

Understanding the different types of insurance providers can assist you in navigating the complex world of insurance and finding the best coverage for your needs. Whether you choose a traditional insurance company, a government program, or a specialized provider, it's essential to review policies carefully, compare quotes, and consider factors like reputation, customer service, and financial stability before making your decision. Remember, insurance is a vital tool for protecting yourself, your loved ones, and your assets, so invest the time and effort to make the right choice for your peace of mind.

Researching and Comparing Insurance Companies

Insurance plays a crucial role in protecting what matters most in life. However, choosing the right one can be overwhelming for many insurance companies. This subchapter aims to guide you through researching and comparing insurance companies, ensuring you make an informed decision.

The first step in researching insurance companies is to assess your individual needs. Determine what kind of coverage you require- auto, home, life, or any other type. Understanding your requirements will help you narrow down the list of potential insurers.

Once you have identified your requirements, it's time to start your research. Begin by gathering information about different insurance companies. Visit their websites, read customer reviews, and explore their social media presence. Look for companies with a positive reputation for excellent customer service and prompt claims processing.

In addition to online research, it is essential to reach out to friends, family, and colleagues with insurance company experience. Their recommendations can provide valuable insights and help you make a more informed decision.

While researching, watch for the financial stability of the insurance companies you are considering. Look for their credit ratings from reputable rating agencies such as Standard & Poor's or A. M. Best. A financially stable company is more likely to honour claims and provide long-term coverage.

As you narrow down your options, compare the coverage and prices different insurers offer. Ensure you understand each policy's terms and conditions, deductibles, and limits. Consider requesting quotes from multiple companies to understand the cost variations better.

Examining the claims process and the company's track record in handling claims is also crucial. A company with a reputation for quick and fair claims settlement is an excellent choice.

Finally, consider the customer service and support provided by the insurance companies. Evaluate their accessibility, responsiveness, and availability of online tools and resources. A company prioritising customer satisfaction will likely be reliable in the long run.

By thoroughly researching and comparing insurance companies, you can make an informed decision that aligns with your needs. Insurance is a long-term commitment, so choosing the right company is worth the effort.

State and Federal Regulations in Insurance

Regarding insurance, various state and federal regulations are in place to ensure policyholders' protection and fair treatment. Understanding these regulations is crucial for insurance providers and consumers to navigate the complex world of insurance.

At the state level, each state has its own insurance department or regulatory body responsible for overseeing insurance activities within its jurisdiction. These departments enforce laws and regulations that govern insurance companies, agents, and policies. They ensure that insurance providers are financially stable, adhere to ethical practices, and provide fair coverage to policyholders.

State regulations cover many areas, including licensing requirements for insurance agents, consumer protection laws, rate regulation, and claim handling procedures. Licensing requirements ensure that insurance agents are knowledgeable and qualified to sell insurance products. Consumer protection laws safeguard policyholders from unfair practices, such as deceptive advertising or improper denial of claims.   Rate regulation ensures that insurance premiums are reasonable and not excessive.   Finally,   claim handling procedures set guidelines for how insurance companies should take, and process claims effectively and efficiently.

On the other hand, federal regulations play a vital role in insurance oversight, particularly in areas where states lack authority. The primary federal agency responsible for insurance regulation is the Federal Insurance Office (FIO).   The FIO monitors the insurance industry,   identifies insurance market issues, and advises the U. S. Treasury on insurance matters. Federal laws such as the Employee Retirement Income Security Act (ERISA) and the Affordable Care Act (ACA) have significantly impacted health insurance regulation.

While state and federal regulations aim to protect policyholders, they also provide a framework for insurance businesses to operate smoothly. Insurance providers can build trust and credibility with their customers by complying with these regulations. Likewise, consumers can be confident that their insurance policies are backed by a regulated industry prioritising their interests.

In conclusion, state and federal regulations in insurance are essential for ensuring a fair and transparent industry. These regulations protect consumers, set standards for insurance providers, and promote the overall stability of the insurance market. Whether you are an insurance professional or a policyholder, understanding these regulations is critical to making informed decisions and navigating the insurance landscape successfully.

Understanding Insurance Policies and Legal Contracts

Insurance is a crucial aspect of our lives that provides protection and peace of mind in times of uncertainty. Understanding the policies and legal contracts involved is vital, whether health, auto, home, or life insurance. This subchapter will delve into the intricacies of insurance policies and legal agreements, ensuring a comprehensive understanding of these essential documents.

Insurance policies serve as written agreements between the insured and the insurance company. They outline the insurance plan's terms, conditions, and coverage details. These policies are legal contracts that establish the rights and responsibilities of both parties involved. It is crucial to carefully read and comprehend the policy before signing it to ensure you know what is covered and what is not.

One of the vital elements of insurance policies is the coverage. Each policy specifies the risks or events that the insurance company covers. Not all risks may be covered, so it is crucial to thoroughly read the policy to understand the extent of protection provided. Additionally, policies may contain exclusions, specific circumstances, or uncovered events. Understanding these exclusions is essential to avoid any surprises when filing a claim.

Insurance policies also outline the obligations and responsibilities of the insured. This may include paying premiums on time, providing accurate information during the application process, and promptly notifying the insurance company in case of a claim. Failure to meet these obligations may result in the denial of coverage or reduced benefits.

Legal contracts form the foundation of insurance policies. They establish both parties' legal rights and obligations and provide a framework for resolving disputes. Legal agreements are designed to protect the interests of all parties involved and ensure fair and equitable treatment.

In conclusion, understanding insurance policies and legal contracts is crucial for anyone seeking insurance coverage. These documents outline the insurance plan's terms, conditions, and coverage details, establishing the rights and responsibilities of the insured and the insurance company. By familiarizing yourself with the policy, you can make informed decisions and ensure adequate protection in times of need.

Chapter 6

Insurance Premiums and Payments

Factors Affecting Insurance Premiums

When it comes to insurance, understanding the factors that influence your premiums is crucial. Insurance premiums are the payments you make to an insurance company in exchange for coverage and protection against potential risks. However, these premiums are not set arbitrarily. Insurance companies consider various factors when determining the cost of your coverage. In this subchapter, we will explore the key factors that affect insurance premiums, providing a better understanding of how these calculations are made.

One primary factor impacting insurance premiums is your risk profile. Insurance companies assess the level of risk associated with insuring you based on several factors, such as age, gender, occupation, and lifestyle choices. For example, younger individuals may face higher premiums due to their perceived higher risk of accidents or health issues. Similarly, certain occupations, such as those involving manual labour or hazardous environments, can also increase premiums.

Your medical history and overall health also significantly determine insurance premiums, especially for health and life insurance. Insurance companies evaluate pre-existing conditions, family medical history, and lifestyle habits like smoking or excessive alcohol consumption. These factors can affect the likelihood of claims and their potential associated costs.

Another significant factor is the type and level of coverage you choose. Different insurance policies offer varying degrees of protection, the more comprehensive the coverage, the higher the premiums. For example, the liability coverage, deductible, and additional coverage options in auto insurance all contribute to the final premium cost. Similarly, in home insurance, factors like coverage limits, deductibles, and the value of the insured property influence the premiums.

Additionally, external factors beyond your control can impact insurance premiums. These include the local crime rate, natural disasters prevalent in your area, or even the overall economic conditions. Insurance companies consider these factors when estimating the likelihood of claims being made and adjust the premiums accordingly.

Understanding the factors that affect insurance premiums is essential for making informed decisions regarding your coverage. By being aware of these factors, you can take steps to minimize risks, such as improving your health or maintaining a safe driving record. Moreover, comparing different insurance providers and policies can help you find the best coverage at affordable premium rates.

Remember, insurance premiums are not set in stone and can be influenced by various factors. Therefore, it is essential to regularly review your policies, reassess your risk profile, and explore different options to ensure you are getting the best value for your insurance coverage.

Different Payment Options for Insurance

When purchasing insurance, it is essential to consider the various payment options available to you. Insurance companies understand that everyone has different financial situations and offer flexible payment plans to accommodate multiple needs. In this subchapter, we will explore the other payment options for insurance, empowering you to make an informed decision.

One of the most common payment options is the annual payment plan. With this option, you pay your insurance premium in full for the entire year upfront. This approach often discounts the overall insurance cost, as insurance companies reward customers for paying in advance. However, it may require a larger initial payment, which may not be feasible for everyone.

For those who prefer a smaller upfront payment, there is the option of a semi-annual payment plan. With this option, you divide your total premium into two instalments, payable every six months. While this may result in a slightly higher overall cost due to administrative fees, it allows for a more manageable payment schedule.

Another popular option is the quarterly payment plan. This approach allows you to pay your insurance premium in four equal instalments annually. While it offers more flexibility than an annual or semi-annual plan, it may incur additional fees and slightly higher costs.

Some insurance companies also offer monthly payment plans. This option allows you to spread your premium over twelve months, making equal payments each month. While this may be the most convenient option for many individuals, it often comes with higher administrative fees—additionally, ensure sufficient funds in your account each month to cover the payment.

It is worth mentioning that some insurance companies offer discounts for customers who opt for automatic payment plans. You can avoid missing due dates and potentially encountering late fees by setting up automatic payments.

Before selecting a payment option, reviewing your budget and assessing which plan aligns with your financial situation is essential. Consider factors such as the overall cost, convenience, and potential discounts. By understanding the various payment options, you can choose the one that best suits your needs while protecting your valuable assets with insurance coverage.

Insurance is an investment in your peace of mind and financial security. Therefore, choosing a payment plan that protects what matters most to you without straining your finances is crucial.

Strategies for Reducing Insurance Premiums

Insurance is essential to our lives, offering protection and peace of mind in the face of unexpected events. However, it's no secret that insurance premiums can sometimes strain our wallets. That is why it is essential to understand the various strategies available for reducing insurance premiums. This subchapter will explore practical tactics to help you save money on insurance policies.

1. Comparison Shopping: One of the most effective ways to reduce insurance premiums is by shopping around and comparing quotes

from different insurance providers. Doing so lets you find the best coverage at the most affordable price. Online platforms make obtaining multiple quotes and comparing coverage options more accessible.

2. Bundle Your Policies: Many insurance companies offer discounts when you bundle multiple policies together. For example, if you have homeowners and auto insurance, consider combining them under one provider. Bundling simplifies your insurance management and can lead to significant savings.

3. Increase Deductibles: Raising your deductible is another strategy to reduce insurance premiums. A deductible is paid out of pocket before your insurance coverage kicks in. You assume more risk by opting for a higher deductible, but your premiums will likely decrease. However, ensure you can afford the deductible in case of a claim.

4. Improve Security Measures: If you have home insurance, installing security systems such as burglar alarms, smoke detectors, and fire extinguishers can lead to premium reductions. Similarly, equipping your vehicle with anti-theft devices or taking

defensive driving courses may lower your auto insurance premiums.

5. Maintain a Good Credit Score: Believe it or not, your credit score can impact your insurance premiums. Insurance companies often use credit scores to assess risk levels. Maintaining a good credit score by paying bills on time and managing debt responsibly can help you secure lower premiums.

6. Regularly Review Your Coverage: As your circumstances change, so do your insurance needs. Periodically review your policies to ensure you are not over insured or underinsured. Adjusting your coverage accordingly can help you avoid paying unnecessary premiums.

By implementing these strategies, you can effectively reduce your insurance premiums without compromising the level of protection you receive. Remember, staying informed and regularly reassessing your insurance needs is crucial to ensure you get the best value for your money.

Chapter 7

Managing Insurance Policies

Reviewing and Updating Insurance Policies

One of the most vital aspects of maintaining a comprehensive insurance plan is regularly reviewing and updating your insurance policies. Life is constantly changing, and with these changes come new risks and needs that must be addressed to ensure proper coverage. This subchapter will guide you through the importance of reviewing and updating your insurance policies, providing valuable insights for all individuals seeking insurance protection.

Insurance policies are designed to safeguard individuals, families, and businesses from unforeseen events that could result in financial loss. However, failing to review and update these policies regularly can leave you vulnerable to gaps in coverage or paying for unnecessary protection. Life is full of changes, such as the purchase of new assets, changes in personal circumstances, or evolving risks in our world. All of these factors can impact the adequacy of your insurance coverage.

Reviewing your insurance policies periodically ensures that you have adequate coverage for your current needs. Start by assessing changes in your life, such as marriage, divorce, childbirth, or purchasing a new home or vehicle. These events often require adjustments to your insurance policies to provide the appropriate level of protection. Additionally, consider any changes in your financial situation, as this can impact the coverage you need.

It is important to note that insurance policies can also become outdated due to changes in regulations or advancements in industry practices. Reviewing your policies periodically allows you to take advantage of new offerings and enhancements that may be available. Insurance providers often update their policies to better align with emerging risks and provide more comprehensive coverage. By staying up to date, you can ensure that you are taking advantage of the latest advancements in the insurance industry.

Furthermore, reviewing and updating your insurance policies can also result in potential cost savings. You may be eligible for discounts or lower premiums as your circumstances change. For example, if you have installed security systems in your home or have completed defensive driving courses, you may qualify for reduced rates on your homeowner's insurance or auto insurance.

In conclusion, reviewing and updating your insurance policies is essential to ensure adequate coverage for your evolving needs and to take advantage of any cost savings opportunities. By staying informed and proactive in managing your insurance, you can protect yourself, your family, and your assets from unexpected events and financial loss.

Adding or Removing Coverage

Insurance policies are designed to provide protection and peace of mind in various aspects of our lives. However, as our circumstances change, so do our insurance needs. This subchapter will guide you through adding or removing coverage, ensuring your insurance policy aligns with your current situation.

Adding Coverage:

Life is unpredictable, and assessing regularly whether your insurance coverage adequately meets your needs is essential. When considering adding coverage, there are a few key factors to consider. First and foremost, evaluate any significant life changes, such as getting married, having children, or purchasing a new home. These milestones often require additional coverage to protect your loved ones and assets.

Furthermore, assess your current policy to determine any gaps in coverage. For example, suppose you own valuable items such as artwork, jewellery, or collectables. In that case, you may need to add a separate policy or endorse your existing policy to ensure they are adequately protected. Additionally, if you have recently started a business or acquired new vehicles, it is essential to update your policies accordingly.

Removing Coverage:

On the other hand, there may be instances where removing coverage is necessary. As your circumstances change, certain risks may no longer apply to you. For example, if your children have moved out and are financially independent, you may consider removing coverage related to their education or dependent care.

Similarly, if you have paid off your mortgage, you may no longer require mortgage protection insurance. However, it is crucial to consult your insurance agent or financial advisor before making any decisions. They can guide you through the potential consequences of removing coverage and help you make an informed choice.

Reviewing and Updating:

Regularly reviewing and updating your insurance policies is vital to protect you. You are conducting an annual review of your insurance coverage, or a biennial review is recommended. This review should include an assessment of your circumstances, assets, and any potential changes that may have occurred during the previous year.

Remember, insurance is designed to provide financial protection against unforeseen events. By adding or removing coverage as needed, you can ensure that your policy remains relevant and practical. Consult a licensed insurance professional to guide you through this process and help you make informed decisions.

Renewing Insurance Policies

In the ever-changing landscape of the insurance industry, individuals must stay informed about their insurance policies and understand the importance of renewing them promptly. This subchapter sheds light on restoring insurance policies, their significance, and the potential consequences of failing them. Whether you are a seasoned insurance policyholder or a newcomer to the insurance world, this section will provide you with valuable insights to confidently navigate the renewal process.

Renewing an insurance policy involves extending the coverage period beyond the initial term. It is important to remember that insurance policies are not indefinite and typically have a set duration, usually one year. As the expiration date approaches, policyholders receive renewal notices from their insurance providers, outlining the terms and conditions for the upcoming policy period. These notices often contain information on any changes to the policy, including premium adjustments, coverage modifications, or additional options.

Understanding the significance of renewing insurance policies is essential for maintaining adequate protection. Renewal offers an opportunity to reassess your coverage needs and make adjustments accordingly. Your insurance needs may evolve as life circumstances change, such as buying a new car, moving to a new house, or starting a family. Failing to renew your policy or neglecting the renewal notice can result in a lapse in coverage, leaving you vulnerable to financial loss in the event of an accident, theft, or other covered incidents.

To ensure a smooth insurance renewal process, it is advisable to review your policy thoroughly. Take the time to assess your current coverage, compare it with other available options in the market, and consider consulting with an insurance professional if needed. This step will enable you to make informed decisions about your insurance needs and potentially identify opportunities for cost savings or enhanced coverage.

Additionally, paying attention to the timeline specified in the renewal notice is crucial. Most insurance providers require policyholders to renew within a specific timeframe to maintain continuous coverage. Failure to continue within the specified period may result in a more complicated process, such as reapplying for insurance or facing higher premiums due to a break in coverage.

In conclusion, renewing insurance policies is critical to maintaining adequate protection and staying financially secure. By understanding the renewal process, reviewing your coverage, and acting within the specified timeframe, you can ensure a seamless transition from one policy period to another. Stay vigilant, stay informed, and renew your insurance policies promptly to safeguard your peace of mind and protect your most valuable assets.

Cancelling Insurance Policies

In the dynamic world of insurance, circumstances may arise that require policyholders to cancel their insurance policies. Understanding the process and implications of cancelling insurance policies is essential, whether due to changing needs, financial constraints, or simply finding a better coverage option. This subchapter aims to provide a comprehensive guide on cancelling insurance policies, addressing the concerns of the general audience and individuals within the insurance niche.

1.   Reasons for Cancelling Insurance Policies:

- Changing coverage needs: As life evolves, individuals may require different types or levels of insurance coverage.

-    Financial considerations: Budget adjustments may prompt policyholders to reevaluate their insurance expenses.

- Better alternatives: Discovering more suitable insurance policies or providers can be a valid reason to cancel existing coverage.

2. Cancelling Process:

- Review the policy terms: Carefully examine the policy documents to understand cancellation provisions, notice periods, and potential penalties.

- Communicate with the insurer: Notify the insurance company in writing about the intent to cancel the policy, specifying the effective cancellation date.

- Pro-rated refunds: In many cases, policyholders are entitled to a refund for the unused portion of their premiums.

3. Implications of Cancelling:

- Coverage gaps: Cancelling a policy without securing an alternative coverage plan may leave individuals unprotected against potential risks.

- Future insurability: A history of policy cancellations may affect future insurance applications, as insurers could see it as a red flag.

- Refund considerations: Policies are generally refundable, but it's essential to understand any cancellation fees or penalties that may reduce the refund amount.

4. Seeking Professional Advice:

- Insurance agents or brokers: Seeking guidance from insurance professionals can help navigate the complexities of cancelling policies and finding suitable alternatives.

- Financial advisors: Consulting with a financial advisor can provide valuable insights into the financial implications of policy cancellations.

Remember, cancelling insurance policies should be done thoughtfully and after careful consideration of the consequences. Evaluating the coverage needs, comparing alternatives, and seeking professional advice when necessary is advisable. By understanding the process and implications of cancelling insurance policies, individuals can make informed decisions that align with their changing circumstances and provide ongoing protection.

Chapter 8

Insurance for Different Life Stages

Insurance for Young Adults

As young adults embark on their journey into the real world, there are many responsibilities they must shoulder, and one of the most important is protecting themselves against unforeseen risks. Insurance becomes a vital aspect of their lives, providing financial security and peace of mind. In this subchapter, we will explore the various types of insurance that young adults should consider and how it can benefit them in different aspects of their lives.

Health insurance is a top priority for young adults, as it ensures access to quality healthcare without the burden of excessive medical bills. With the rising cost of medical treatments, having health insurance coverage can be a lifesaver in times of illness or injury. Promoting preventive care and routine check-ups helps young adults maintain their overall well-being.

Another crucial insurance policy for young adults is auto insurance. As they venture into the world of driving, having vehicle coverage is not only a legal requirement but also a means to protect themselves and others on the road. Auto insurance safeguards against potential damages, accidents, or thefts, providing financial support when needed most.

Young adults often overlook Renter's insurance when they move into their first apartments. However, protecting the belongings from theft, fire, or natural disasters is essential. It also provides liability coverage if someone is injured in their rented space. Renter's insurance is a cost-effective way to safeguard valuable possessions and provide financial support in challenging situations.

Life insurance may not be a priority for young adults, but it is an investment that can provide long-term benefits. It offers financial protection to loved ones during a tragic loss, covering funeral expenses and outstanding debts or providing financial stability for dependents.

Lastly, young adults should consider disability insurance, which protects against loss of income due to disability or injury, ensuring they can still meet their financial obligations even if they cannot work. This type of insurance is essential for those with student loans or other financial responsibilities.

In conclusion, insurance is essential to a young adult's life, providing protection and financial security in various parts. Health insurance, auto insurance, renter's insurance, life insurance, and disability insurance are all crucial policies to consider. By understanding the importance of insurance and making informed decisions, young adults can navigate life's uncertainties with confidence and peace of mind.

Insurance for Couples and Families

Insurance is crucial in protecting your loved ones and ensuring their financial security. As a couple or a family, it is essential to understand the various insurance options available to you and how they can safeguard your future. This subchapter will provide a comprehensive guide on insurance for couples and families, helping you make informed decisions for your loved ones' well-being.

Life insurance is one of the most fundamental types of insurance for couples and families. Life insurance provides a financial safety net in the event of an untimely death. It ensures that your family members are cared for by providing them with a lump sum or regular payments to cover mortgage payments, education costs, and daily living expenses. Understanding the different types of life insurance, such as term and whole life insurance, will help you choose the most suitable coverage for your family's needs.

Health insurance is another vital aspect of protecting your family's well-being. It offers financial coverage for medical expenses, ensuring you and your loved ones can receive quality healthcare without excessive costs. When selecting a health insurance plan that meets your family's specific requirements, it is essential to consider coverage limits, deductibles, and network providers.

Homeowners or renters' insurance is an indispensable form of protection for couples and families. This insurance covers your property and possessions against unforeseen events such as fire, theft, or natural disasters. It provides financial reimbursement for repairs, replacements, and liability claims, allowing you to maintain the security and stability of your home.

Additionally, auto insurance is a must-have for families with vehicles. It protects you and your loved ones from financial losses from accidents, theft, or vehicle damage. Understanding different coverage options, such as liability, collision, and comprehensive coverage, will help you select the most suitable policy for your family's needs.

Lastly, consider umbrella insurance, which provides an extra layer of liability coverage beyond the limits of your primary insurance policies. This coverage mainly benefits families, protecting your assets and future income from unexpected lawsuits or liability claims.

By understanding the importance of insurance for couples and families and exploring the various coverage options available, you can make informed decisions to protect your loved ones. Review your insurance policies periodically and adjust them as your family's needs evolve. With the right insurance coverage, you can have peace of mind knowing that you have taken the necessary steps to secure your family's financial future.

Insurance for Retirees and Seniors

As we enter our golden years, ensuring we have the right insurance coverage to protect ourselves and our loved ones becomes increasingly essential. Retirement brings new challenges and considerations; having the appropriate insurance can provide peace of mind and financial security. In this subchapter, we will explore the various types of insurance that are particularly relevant to retirees and seniors.

One of the most crucial insurance policies for this demographic is health insurance. As we age, the likelihood of developing health issues increases, and having comprehensive coverage can help offset the costs of medical treatments, prescription drugs, and hospital stays. Medicare is a federal health insurance program available to individuals 65 or older but may not cover all expenses. Supplemental insurance, such as Medigap or Medicare Advantage plans, can bridge the gaps in coverage and provide additional benefits.

Another essential insurance policy for retirees and seniors is long-term care insurance. This coverage helps pay for the costs associated with care in a nursing home, assisted living facility, or at home. Long-term care can be costly; without insurance, these costs can quickly deplete one's savings. Obtaining this coverage while still in good health is advisable, as premiums tend to be lower and eligibility requirements more lenient.

Life insurance is another consideration for retirees and seniors. While the need for life insurance may decrease as dependents grow older and financial obligations fall, it can still serve as a valuable financial tool. Life insurance can provide a death benefit to help cover funeral expenses and outstanding debts or leave a financial legacy for loved ones.

Additionally, older individuals may want to explore travel insurance. Retirement often presents opportunities for travel and exploration, but unforeseen circumstances, such as medical emergencies or trip cancellations, can occur. Travel insurance can cover medical expenses abroad, trip interruption, lost baggage, and other travel-related incidents.

Lastly, retirees and seniors should review their homeowner's insurance and consider adding additional coverage specific to their needs. This can include protection against natural disasters, liability coverage, or coverage for valuable possessions such as jewellery or artwork.

In conclusion, insurance protects retirees and seniors from unexpected financial burdens. Health insurance, long-term care insurance, life insurance, travel insurance, and enhanced homeowner's insurance are all policies that should be carefully considered and tailored to individual needs. By understanding the various types of insurance available and seeking appropriate coverage, retirees and seniors can enjoy their golden years with peace of mind and financial security.

Insurance Considerations for Business Owners

As a business owner, it is crucial to understand the insurance options available to protect your enterprise. This subchapter will delve into the essential insurance considerations every business owner should know. Whether a small business owner or a seasoned entrepreneur, having the right insurance coverage can provide peace of mind and protect your investment from unforeseen circumstances.

One of the primary insurance options for business owners is liability insurance. This coverage safeguards your business from legal claims and financial losses if someone is injured on your premises or your products or services cause harm. Liability insurance can also protect you from legal expenses and settlements in case of lawsuits.

Another essential consideration is property insurance, which covers your physical assets, including your building, equipment, inventory, and furniture, against damage or loss due to fire, theft, vandalism, or natural disasters. Property insurance ensures your business can recover and continue operations even after a significant setback.

In addition to liability and property insurance, business interruption insurance is worth considering. This coverage helps you recover lost income and cover ongoing expenses if your business is temporarily unable to operate due to a covered event, such as a fire or flood. Business interruption insurance can be a lifeline during challenging times, allowing you to maintain financial stability until you can resume normal operations.

For businesses with employees, workers' compensation insurance is essential. This coverage provides medical benefits and wage replacement to employees who are injured or become ill while on the job. Workers' compensation protects your employees and shields your business from potential lawsuits related to workplace injuries.

Lastly, depending on your industry and specific circumstances, there may be other insurance considerations to explore. These could include professional liability insurance, product liability insurance, cyber liability insurance, and commercial auto insurance, among others. It is crucial to assess your unique business needs and consult with an insurance professional to ensure you have comprehensive coverage tailored to your business.

In conclusion, as a business owner, understanding and carefully considering your insurance options is vital for protecting your investment and ensuring the continuity of your operations. Liability insurance, property insurance, business interruption insurance, and workers' compensation insurance are some essential coverage types to explore. By securing the right insurance policies, you can safeguard your business, employees, and financial stability, providing you with the peace of mind to focus on growing and thriving in your industry.

Chapter 9

Insurance and Financial Planning

Aligning Insurance with Financial Goals

Insurance plays a crucial role in safeguarding our financial well-being and protecting us from unexpected events that can disrupt our lives. However, many often overlook the importance of aligning their insurance policies with long-term financial goals. This subchapter will explore the significance of integrating insurance plans with your financial objectives and how they can contribute to your financial security.

Regarding insurance, it's vital to consider your financial goals and aspirations. Whether you aim to save for retirement, purchase a home, fund your child's education, or start a business, insurance can be a valuable tool in helping you achieve these objectives. By strategically aligning insurance with your financial goals, you can create a robust safety net that provides protection and growth opportunities.

A comprehensive coverage evaluation is critical to aligning insurance with financial goals. Assess your insurance policies, including life, health, disability, home, and auto insurance, to ensure they adequately protect your economic interests. Regularly reviewing and updating your coverage is essential, as your circumstances and goals may change over time.

Furthermore, it is crucial to consider the potential risks that could hinder your progress towards your financial goals. For example, if you are the primary breadwinner of your family and your objective is to provide financial stability for your loved ones, a life insurance policy can ensure they are protected in the event of your untimely demise. Similarly, disability insurance can safeguard your income if you cannot work due to an accident or illness.

Additionally, integrating insurance and financial goals involves exploring investment opportunities that align with your risk tolerance and long-term objectives. Specific insurance policies, such as whole life or universal life insurance, offer a cash value component that can accumulate over time and provide a source of funds for future expenses or as an additional retirement savings vehicle.

By aligning insurance with your financial goals, you can create a comprehensive and customized strategy that addresses your short-term protection needs and long-term economic aspirations. Remember to consult with a qualified financial advisor or insurance professional who can help you navigate the complexities of insurance and tailor a plan that fits your unique circumstances.

In conclusion, insurance should not be viewed as a standalone product but as a crucial component of your financial plan. You can ensure immediate protection and long-term financial security by aligning insurance with your financial goals. Remember, the right insurance coverage can provide peace of mind and enable you to pursue your dreams confidently.

Importance of Regular Financial Assessments

In our fast-paced world, it is easy to get caught up in the day-to-day tasks and forget about the bigger picture. When it comes to our finances, this can be a costly mistake. Regular financial assessments are essential to ensure we are adequately protected and prepared for unforeseen circumstances. This subchapter will explore the importance of conducting regular economic assessments, specifically within insurance.

Insurance serves as a safety net, protecting us from potential financial disasters. However, our needs change as we go through different stages of life. Regular economic assessments help determine if our insurance coverage suits our current situation. By assessing our financial goals, liabilities, and assets, we can identify gaps in our coverage and make necessary adjustments.

One of the key benefits of conducting regular financial assessments is identifying potential risks and mitigating them proactively. Life is unpredictable, and we cannot foresee when an accident, illness, or natural disaster might strike. Reviewing our insurance policies ensures adequate coverage for potential risks, such as health, property, or liability issues. This way, we can avoid being underinsured or paying for unnecessary coverage, saving money and stress in the long run.

Furthermore, regular financial assessments empower individuals to take control of their financial future. Assessing our financial situation allows us to set realistic goals, such as saving for retirement, purchasing a home, or funding our children's education. By understanding our income, expenses, and overall financial health, we can make informed decisions about budgeting, investing, and saving.

Regular financial assessments are even more crucial for those who are self-employed or own a business. As entrepreneurs, we face unique risks and responsibilities. Regularly assessing our financial situation ensures we have the appropriate business insurance coverage to protect our assets and operations. Additionally, it allows us to evaluate our business's financial performance and make necessary adjustments to ensure its long-term success.

In conclusion, regular financial assessments are vital for everyone, regardless of their stage in life or occupation. They provide individuals with a clear understanding of their financial situation, help identify potential risks, and enable them to make informed decisions about insurance coverage. By assessing our finances regularly, we can protect ourselves, our loved ones, and our assets, ensuring a secure and prosperous future.

Integrating Insurance into Retirement Planning

Retirement planning is a crucial aspect of every individual's financial journey. As we work hard to secure a comfortable retirement, we must consider all the potential risks and uncertainties that may arise in our later years. This is where insurance plays a vital role in providing protection and peace of mind during retirement.

Regarding retirement planning, insurance can protect against unexpected events that may otherwise derail your financial goals. It acts as a safety net, ensuring you and your loved ones are financially secure despite unforeseen circumstances.

One of the critical aspects of integrating insurance into retirement planning is securing adequate health insurance coverage. As we age, the risk of developing health issues increases significantly. Medical expenses can be exorbitant; without proper health insurance, these costs can quickly deplete your retirement savings. By having comprehensive health insurance coverage, you can safeguard your retirement funds from being eroded by medical bills, ensuring your savings last longer.

Another crucial insurance component to consider is long-term care insurance. As we age, the likelihood of requiring assistance with daily activities such as bathing, dressing, or moving around increases. Long-term care insurance covers the costs associated with nursing homes, assisted living facilities, or in-home care services. By incorporating long-term care insurance into your retirement plan, you can protect your assets from being exhausted due to the high costs of long-term care.

Furthermore, life insurance should also be a part of your retirement planning strategy. Although it may seem counterintuitive to purchase life insurance during retirement, it can serve multiple purposes. Life insurance can provide a source of income for your spouse or beneficiaries in the event of your passing, ensuring they are not burdened financially. Additionally, it can be used as an estate planning tool, allowing you to leave a legacy or cover any potential estate taxes.

In conclusion, integrating insurance into retirement planning is crucial in ensuring a secure and worry-free retirement. By incorporating health insurance, long-term care insurance, and life insurance into your overall retirement strategy, you can protect your savings, mitigate risks, and provide financial security for yourself and your loved ones. Remember, proper insurance coverage can significantly affect how well you enjoy your golden years, so don't overlook its importance in your retirement planning endeavours.

Chapter 10

Insurance Fraud and Scams

Types of Insurance Fraud

Insurance fraud is a serious crime that affects both insurance companies and policyholders. It involves intentionally deceiving an insurance company to obtain financial benefits. Insurance fraud can take various forms, and individuals must be aware of the different types to protect themselves and their insurance policies.

1. Staged Accidents: One common type of insurance fraud is staging accidents to make false insurance claims. Fraudsters may deliberately cause car accidents or fake injuries to claim compensation from their insurance companies. These individuals often collaborate to create false witnesses and evidence to support their claims.

2. False Claims: Insurance policies cover various aspects of life, including health, property, and liability. Some individuals

may file false claims by exaggerating the extent of their injuries or damages. For instance, an individual may claim compensation for lost items, not stolen or damaged.

3. Premium Fraud: Premium fraud occurs when individuals or businesses provide false information to insurance companies to obtain lower premiums. They may misrepresent their occupation, driving history, or the purpose of their property to get a lower premium rate. This type of fraud affects the insurance company and poses a risk to other policyholders, who may pay higher premiums.

4. Identity Theft: Identity theft is a growing concern in the digital age. Fraudsters may steal someone's personal information, such as their social security number or medical records, to file fraudulent insurance claims. This can lead to financial loss and damage to the victim's reputation.

5. Arson Fraud: Arson fraud involves deliberately setting fire to property to collect insurance money. Fraudsters may burn down their homes or businesses and then file claims for the damages caused by the fire. This type

of fraud not only puts lives at risk but also leads to increased insurance premiums for everyone.

Insurance fraud is a serious offence with severe consequences, including fines and imprisonment. Individuals must be vigilant and report suspicious activities to their insurance providers. On the other hand, insurance companies must invest in fraud detection systems and educate their policyholders about the risks and consequences of insurance fraud.

By understanding the different types of insurance fraud, individuals can take necessary precautions to protect themselves and their insurance policies. This knowledge empowers policyholders to make informed decisions and helps insurance companies identify and prevent fraudulent activities, ensuring a fair and sustainable insurance system for everyone.

Recognizing and Avoiding Insurance Scams

This subchapter will explore the importance of recognizing and avoiding insurance scams. Insurance plays a vital role in our lives, providing financial protection and peace of mind. However, there are unscrupulous individuals and organizations out there who seek to take advantage of unsuspecting policyholders. By understanding the common red flags and learning how to protect yourself, you can ensure that you are making informed decisions regarding insurance.

Knowing the warning signs is one of the most crucial steps in avoiding insurance scams. If an offer sounds too good to be true, it probably is. Beware of policies that promise unusually high returns or coverage at a significantly lower cost than other reputable insurers. Additionally, be cautious of aggressive sales tactics, such as high-pressure sales pitches or a limited time offer that pressures you to make a quick decision.

Research is vital when it comes to insurance. Always verify the insurance company's or agent's legitimacy before making payments or signing contracts. Check if your state's insurance department licenses and regulates the insurer. You can also review their ratings and customer reviews to gauge their reputation and reliability. Remember, reputable insurance providers will always be transparent about their credentials and encourage you to do your due diligence.

Be wary of unsolicited calls, emails, or letters offering insurance coverage. Scammers often use these methods to target potential victims. Avoid sharing personal or financial information unless you are confident about the source's legitimacy. If you're unsure, don't hesitate to contact your state insurance department or seek advice from a trusted insurance professional.

Staying informed about the latest insurance scams is crucial in protecting yourself. Regularly visit the websites of reputable insurance organizations and consumer protection agencies to keep up to date with the latest fraud schemes. These resources often provide valuable tips and information on recognising and reporting insurance scams.

Remember, being proactive and cautious is the best defence against insurance scams. By recognizing the warning signs, conducting thorough research, and staying informed, you can safeguard yourself and your hard-earned money from falling victim to fraudulent insurance practices.

In conclusion, insurance scams significantly threaten individuals seeking insurance coverage. It is essential to be aware of the common warning signs and take necessary precautions to protect yourself. By staying informed, conducting thorough research, and trusting your instincts, you can confidently navigate the insurance landscape, ensuring that you are making informed decisions and receiving the protection you deserve.

Reporting Suspected Fraudulent Activities

Fraudulent activities pose a significant threat to the insurance industry and can have severe consequences for insurance companies and policyholders. Individuals must be aware of the signs of potential fraud and understand the importance of reporting any suspected fraudulent activities. This subchapter aims to educate the general audience, specifically those interested in insurance, on the steps to take when encountering potentially fraudulent activities.

Insurance fraud can take various forms, including false claims, exaggerated losses, staged accidents, or fake policies. These fraudulent activities have far-reaching implications, leading to increased premiums for honest policyholders and undermining insurance companies' financial stability.

To combat fraud effectively, everyone needs to be vigilant and report any suspicious activities. If you suspect insurance fraud, the first step is to gather as much information as possible. Take note of unusual details, such as statement inconsistencies, suspicious behaviour, or unexplained damages. Document the date, time, location, and any relevant parties involved.

Once you have gathered the necessary information, promptly report your suspicions to the appropriate authorities. This can typically be done by contacting your insurance company's fraud hotline or customer service department. Many insurance companies have dedicated fraud investigation units trained to handle such reports. Alternatively, you can report suspected insurance fraud to your local law enforcement agency or the National Insurance Crime Bureau (NICB).

When reporting suspected fraudulent activities, providing accurate and detailed information is essential. Be prepared to provide any evidence or documentation supporting your suspicions, such as photographs, witness statements, or other relevant materials. Remember to maintain your confidentiality during the reporting process, as your identity may need to be kept anonymous for your protection. You safeguard your interests and contribute to the insurance industry's integrity by reporting suspected fraudulent activities. Your prompt action can help prevent fraudsters from taking advantage of honest policyholders and ensure that insurance remains a reliable protection for everyone.

In conclusion, reporting suspected fraudulent activities is crucial for maintaining the integrity of the insurance industry. By being aware of the signs of potential fraud and promptly reporting any suspicions, individuals can play an active role in preventing fraudulent activities. Remember, insurance fraud affects all policyholders, and together, we can work towards a safer and more secure insurance environment.

Chapter 11

Future Trends in Insurance

Technological Advances in the Insurance Industry

The rapid advancements in technology have had a significant impact on various industries, and the insurance sector is no exception. As we delve into the "Technological Advances in the Insurance Industry subchapter, " we will explore how technology has transformed the insurance landscape, benefiting insurance providers and policyholders.

One of the most prominent advancements in the insurance industry is using artificial intelligence (AI) and machine learning. These technologies have revolutionized the underwriting process by enabling insurers to analyze vast amounts of data and make more accurate risk assessments. AI-powered algorithms can swiftly evaluate an individual's risk profile, leading to more personalized policies and fairer premiums.

Furthermore, the integration of AI has enhanced customer service in the insurance sector. Chatbots and virtual assistants can respond instantly to customer queries, ensuring round-the-clock support. This improves customer satisfaction and streamlines the claims process, enabling policyholders to receive prompt assistance during stressful times.

The advent of the Internet of Things (IoT) has also greatly impacted the insurance industry. With IoT devices such as intelligent sensors, insurers can now monitor and collect real-time data on insured assets. This allows for proactive risk management, as insurers can identify potential issues and provide timely intervention. For instance, IoT-enabled home devices can detect water leaks, fire hazards, or security breaches, enabling insurers to mitigate risks and prevent extensive damage.

Telematics is another technological advancement that has revolutionized the auto insurance sector. By installing telematics devices in vehicles, insurers can gather data on driving behaviour, such as speed, acceleration, and braking patterns. This data enables insurers to assess risk more accurately and offer usage-based insurance policies, rewarding safer drivers with lower premiums.

Additionally, the digitalization of insurance processes has streamlined operations and improved efficiency. Policyholders can now purchase insurance policies online, submit claims electronically, and track the progress of their claims in real time. This convenience saves time and reduces paperwork and administrative costs for insurers.

In conclusion, technological advances in the insurance industry have transformed how policies are underwritten, claims are processed, and customer service is delivered. These advancements, from AI and machine learning to IoT and telematics, have greatly benefited insurance providers and policyholders. As technology continues to evolve, insurance professionals must stay informed and adapt to these changes to leverage the full potential of these advancements for the benefit of their customers and the industry.

Impact of Artificial Intelligence and Automation

In recent years, the insurance industry has witnessed a significant transformation with the advent of artificial intelligence (AI) and automation technologies. These innovations have revolutionized how insurance companies operate, bringing numerous benefits and challenges for insurers and policyholders alike.

One of the critical advantages of AI and automation in the insurance sector is the ability to streamline and enhance various processes. Tasks that were once time-consuming and error-prone can now be automated, increasing efficiency and accuracy in claims processing, underwriting, and risk assessment. This reduces costs for insurance companies and enables them to provide faster and more personalized services to their customers.

AI-powered chatbots and virtual assistants have become increasingly common in the insurance industry, enabling policyholders to obtain real-time assistance and support. These intelligent systems can answer queries, guide policy selection, and even assist in filing claims. By utilizing AI, insurers can offer round-the-clock customer service, ensuring that individuals receive the help they need when needed.

Furthermore, AI and automation have revolutionized risk assessment and underwriting processes. AI algorithms can accurately assess risks and determine appropriate coverage by buying vast amounts of data, including policyholder information, historical claims data, and external factors such as weather patterns. AI enables insurance companies to tailor policies to individual needs, pricing them more accurately and reducing the potential for fraudulent claims.

However, the rise of AI and automation in the insurance industry also brings specific challenges. One such concern is the potential displacement of human workers. As particular tasks become automated, there is a fear that jobs may be lost. However, it is essential to note that AI and automation technologies also create new job opportunities, particularly in data analysis, AI development, and customer service.

Additionally, there are ethical considerations surrounding the use of AI in insurance. Installing AI algorithms to determine premiums and coverage may unintentionally lead to biases or discriminatory practices. Insurers must ensure their AI systems are transparent, fair, and accessible from discrimination.

In conclusion, the impact of artificial intelligence and automation on the insurance industry is profound. These technologies have revolutionised how insurers operate, from improved efficiency and customer service to enhanced risk assessment and underwriting. However, insurers must navigate the challenges associated with AI and automation, ensuring that ethical considerations are upheld, and workers are not adversely affected. By embracing these technologies responsibly, the insurance industry can continue to provide essential protection to individuals and businesses in an increasingly digital world.

Emerging Insurance Products and Services

In today's rapidly evolving world, insurance is discontinuously adapting to meet consumers' needs and demands. With technological advancements and shifts in societal behaviour, new risks and vulnerabilities have emerged, leading to the development of innovative insurance products and services. This subchapter explores the exciting realm of emerging insurance products and services and their potential impact on everyday protection.

1. Cyber Insurance: As our lives become increasingly digitalized, the risk of cyber threats and data breaches has become a significant concern. Cyber insurance covers financial losses from cyber-attacks, such as identity theft, data breaches, and ransomware. Whether you're an individual or a business owner, having cyber insurance can provide peace of mind in an ever-connected world.

2. Usage-Based Insurance (UBI): Traditional auto insurance policies are based on age, gender, and location. However, emerging technologies such as telematics allow insurers to gather data on driving behaviour, offering personalized premiums based on actual usage. UBI incentivizes safe driving habits and provides cost savings for individuals who drive less or exhibit responsible driving behaviour.

3. Insurance for the Sharing Economy: The rise of platforms like Airbnb and Uber has given birth to the sharing economy, where individuals rent out their homes, cars, or other assets. Insurers now offer specialised coverage tailored to these activities to address the unique risks associated with this new economic model. Whether you're a host or a guest, having insurance specifically designed for the sharing economy can protect against liabilities that traditional policies may not cover.

4. Parametric Insurance: Natural disasters like hurricanes and earthquakes can cause significant financial losses. Parametric insurance use's objective, predetermined parameters (e. g. , wind speed or earthquake magnitude) to trigger claim payments. This type of insurance eliminates the need for lengthy claims assessments and provides quicker payouts, aiding in faster recovery.

5. Peer-to-Peer Insurance: Peer-to-peer insurance leverages the power of communities to pool risks and provide coverage at potentially lower costs. Through digital platforms, individuals or small groups can mutually insure one another, creating a sense of shared responsibility and trust. This

innovative approach disrupts the traditional insurance model by empowering individuals to take control of their own insurance needs.

As the insurance landscape evolves, these emerging products and services offer individuals and businesses new avenues for mitigating risks and protecting their assets. Consumers must stay informed and consider these innovative options to ensure they have the most appropriate coverage for their needs. By embracing these emerging insurance products and services, individuals can face the future with greater confidence and peace of mind.

Chapter 12

Conclusion and Further Resources

Recap of Key Insurance Concepts

This subchapter will provide a comprehensive overview and recap of the vital insurance concepts discussed thus far in "The Insurance Handbook: A General Guide for Everyday Protection. " Whether you are a general reader or interested in the insurance industry, this recap will be a valuable resource to reinforce your understanding of essential insurance concepts.

First and foremost, it is crucial to understand the fundamental purpose of insurance. Insurance acts as a safeguard against financial losses that may arise due to unexpected events. Individuals and businesses can protect themselves from potentially devastating economic consequences by transferring the risk to an insurance company.

One of the most critical concepts in insurance is the concept of risk. Risk refers to the likelihood of an event occurring and its potential impact. Insurance companies assess risks based on various factors such as age, health, occupation, and driving history, among others. By understanding how risk is evaluated, individuals can make informed decisions when selecting insurance policies that suit their needs.

Another key concept is the concept of premiums. Premiums are the payments made by policyholders to insurance companies in exchange for coverage. The premium amount is determined by the risk associated with the insured individual or property. It is important to note that premiums can vary depending on factors such as deductibles, coverage limits, and the type of policy chosen.

Furthermore, insurance policies are contracts that outline the terms and conditions of the coverage provided. Policyholders must carefully review and understand the policy language to ensure they know their rights and obligations. Common policy types include life insurance, health insurance, auto insurance, and homeowner's insurance, each designed to address specific risks and provide appropriate protection.

Claims are an integral part of the insurance process. When an insured event occurs, policyholders submit a claim to their insurance company to seek compensation for the losses. The insurance company then evaluates the claim and, if approved, provides the agreed-upon reimbursement or coverage.

Lastly, it is essential to consider the concept of exclusions and limitations within insurance policies. Exclusions are specific events or circumstances not covered by the insurance policy, while limitations refer to the maximum amount an insurance company will pay for a particular claim.

By understanding these key insurance concepts, individuals can make informed decisions when purchasing insurance policies and ensure they are protected against unforeseen events. Whether you are a general reader or have an interest in the insurance industry, this recap serves as a valuable resource for understanding the essential principles of insurance.

Additional Reading and Resources

In the constantly evolving insurance world, staying informed and up-to-date is crucial. This subchapter aims to provide a list of additional reading materials and resources that can serve as valuable references for general audiences and those interested in the insurance industry. Whether you are a policyholder seeking to understand better your coverage or an insurance professional looking to expand your knowledge, these resources will help you confidently navigate the complex insurance landscape.

1. Insurance websites and blogs: Many reputable websites and blogs are dedicated to the insurance industry. These platforms often offer a wealth of information, including articles, guides, and industry news. Some popular insurance websites include Insurance Journal, Risk & Insurance, and the Insurance Information Institute.

2. Online courses and webinars: Various online platforms offer courses and webinars on insurance-related topics, suitable for

beginners and experienced professionals. These interactive learning experiences can help you deepen your knowledge and stay current with industry trends.

Remember, the insurance landscape constantly changes, with new products, regulations, and technologies emerging regularly. Investing time in additional reading and exploring the available resources, you will be better equipped to make informed decisions about your insurance needs and stay ahead of the curve in this dynamic industry.

Seeking Professional Advice in Insurance Matters

In insurance matters, seeking professional advice can make a difference in ensuring you have the right coverage to protect yourself, your loved ones, and your assets. Insurance is a complex field, with various policies, terms, and conditions that can be overwhelming for the general audience. That's why it is crucial to consult with insurance professionals who can guide you through the intricacies of insurance and help you make informed decisions.

Insurance professionals, such as insurance agents or brokers, have extensive knowledge and expertise in the insurance industry. They understand the nuances of different insurance policies and can provide valuable insights tailored to your needs. If you are looking for health, life, auto, or any other type of coverage, seeking professional advice is essential for obtaining the most appropriate and cost-effective insurance solutions.

One of the primary reasons for seeking professional advice is to ensure that you have adequate coverage. Insurance professionals can assess your unique circumstances and recommend the appropriate level of coverage to safeguard your interests. They will consider your age, health condition, financial situation, and risk tolerance to customize insurance plans that meet your requirements.

Moreover, insurance professionals can help you navigate the complex claims process. Dealing with insurance companies can be daunting and time-consuming in the unfortunate event of a claim. However, by seeking professional advice, you can have an expert who will guide you through the process, helping you understand the necessary steps, documentation, and requirements. They can also negotiate to ensure you receive a fair settlement.

Insurance professionals also stay updated with the latest industry trends and regulations. They can educate you about changes in insurance laws, new policies, or emerging risks that may impact your coverage. By staying informed, you proactively adjust your insurance plans, protecting against potential threats.

In conclusion, seeking professional advice in insurance matters is crucial for anyone looking to protect their assets and loved ones. Insurance professionals have the knowledge, expertise, and resources to guide you through the complexities of insurance and ensure you have the right coverage for your specific needs. By consulting with an insurance expert, you can make informed decisions, navigate the claims process more effectively, and stay updated with the ever-changing insurance landscape. So, don't hesitate to seek professional advice and secure your everyday protection.